BRENT LIBRARIES

Please return/renew this item
by the last date shown.
Books may also be renewed by
phone or online.
Tel: 0333 370 4700
On-line www.brent.gov.uk/libraryservice

Science in a flash

Light

Georgia
Amson-Bradshaw

W
FRANKLIN WATTS
LONDON·SYDNEY

Franklin Watts
First published in Great Britain in 2017 by The Watts Publishing Group

Copyright © The Watts Publishing Group 2017

 Produced for Franklin Watts by
White-Thomson Publishing Ltd
www.wtpub.co.uk

Credits
Series Editor: Georgia Amson-Bradshaw
Series Designer: Rocket Design (East Anglia) Ltd

Images from Shutterstock.com: silver tiger 5c, Enmaler 7br, Alhovik 7b, Lisa S. 9t, Wansfordphoto 11t, Zurijeta 12b, Andrea Izzotti 15c, petovarga 15bl, MilanB 16r, Alex Mit 18bl, Asier Romero 20r, Toukung design 22l, Glasscage 22bl, superjoseph 23r
Illustrations by Steve Evans: 4br, 5r, 6b, 8c, 10b, 12c, 13t, 13b, 15b, 17br, 20b, 20t, 21bl, 21b, 21c, 22 br, 24lbl, 26tr.
All design elements from Shutterstock.

HB ISBN 978 1 4451 5206 6
PB ISBN 978 1 4451 5207 3

Printed in China

MIX
Paper from responsible sources
FSC
www.fsc.org
FSC® C104740

Franklin Watts
An imprint of
Hachette Children's Group
Part of The Watts Publishing Group
Carmelite House
50 Victoria Embankment
London EC4Y 0DZ

An Hachette UK Company
www.hachette.co.uk

www.franklinwatts.co.uk

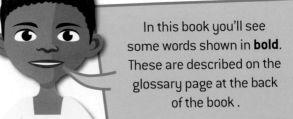

In this book you'll see some words shown in **bold**. These are described on the glossary page at the back of the book .

Contents

WHAT IS LIGHT?

Light is a type of energy.

Every day we are surrounded by light. Even on the darkest night we can usually see a little bit of light, from a twinkling star or a glowing screen. But what actually IS light? And what is it made of? Light is a type of energy, like heat or electricity.

Give us a wave!

Light energy travels in the form of waves. These are like the waves in the sea, but a lot smaller.

Buzz

Scientists also call light **electromagnetic radiation**. This is because a light wave is made up of both electric and magnetic vibrations.

Did you know?

The scientific study of light is called 'optics'. Technology such as digital cameras and wireless computer mice were developed using the science of optics.

4

Wait! There's more ...

However, light waves aren't the end of the story. In some experiments, light behaves more like particles, or bits of stuff. Scientists call these bits of light **photons**.

Can you pass me a particle?

Unlike most 'stuff', photons have no mass. You couldn't collect them in a box. So light isn't quite like anything else. A bit like a wave, and a bit like a particle, light is unique.

Err?

CONTAINS 100% LIGHT

POP QUIZ!

The light you can see isn't the only sort of light. There are other types of electromagnetic waves that our eyes can't detect. **Can you guess which of these three things is NOT a type of light?**

Read more about types of light on pages 24-25. **Answers on page 28**

1. **Microwaves**   2. **Radio waves**   3. **Sound waves**

Sources of Light

Light can be made or reflected.

Some things give out light, like the sun or a torch. These are called 'light sources'. Light sources can be natural, like the sun, or man-made, like a lightbulb. Other things bounce light off them, but do not make it themselves, like the moon. This is called reflecting.

Let there be light!

Light is made when one type of energy is changed into another type. The lightbulbs in your house change electrical energy into light energy. Fire gives off light by changing chemical energy into light energy.

Find the light

How many different light sources can you spot in this picture?

Our super source

Our biggest natural light source is the sun, the star at the centre of our galaxy. A huge ball of burning gas, it lights up the earth from 150 million kilometres away.

Light comes from the sun ...

FACT ATTACK

Who's the daddy?

It's the biggest thing in our solar system, but our sun is quite puny compared to other stars in the universe. Scientist have found a star they have called R136a1 that is 10 million times brighter than our sun!

... Light then bounces off the moon and travels to earth

Moon mirror

Although the moon can look very bright, especially when it is full, it doesn't make its own light, so it isn't a light source. The light we see comes from the sun, and bounces off the moon like a mirror.

Find out more about reflecting on page 14

Light on the move

Light travels very fast in straight lines.

Light is the fastest thing in the universe. It travels incredibly quickly, at 300,000 km per second. This is so fast it seems instant to us. Light from the sun takes only 8 minutes to reach earth – even though it comes from 150 million kilometres away!

Give it a go!

Prove that light travels in straight lines. Collect four pieces of card, and cut a small hole in the centre of three of the pieces. Use some modelling clay to stand the cards vertically in a row. Put the one without a hole at the far end.

Place a bright lamp or torch at the front end of the row of cards. If the holes are all perfectly lined up, a straight beam of light should reach the final card. To best see the effect, do this in a dark room.

Pin hole in card only allows small beam of light through

Modelling clay

Straight forward

Light travels in straight lines, called rays. Rays can spread out, but they can't go around corners. It's sometimes possible to see light spreading out in rays when the sun is shining from behind clouds or mountains.

I've already watched all the in-flight movies and there's still a million years to go...

Light years

Although 150 million kilometres sounds very far, our sun is quite close compared to other things in space. Distances in space can be so big, that they are often measured in light years. This is a measure of distance that is equal to – yep, you guessed it – how far light travels in a year. In comparison, it would take a passenger jet over a million years to travel the same distance.

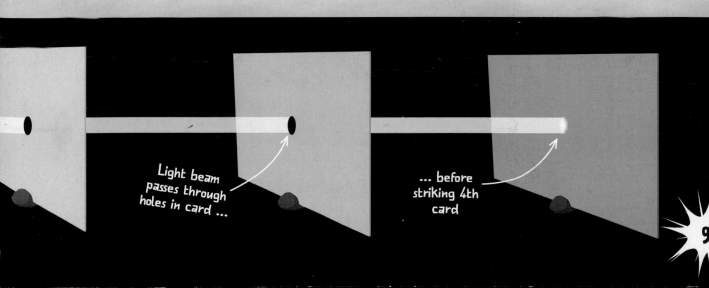

Light beam passes through holes in card ...

... before striking 4th card

LIGHT and MATERIALS

Light can travel through some materials, but not others.

Some materials like wood or brick block light. We call these *materials* **opaque**. *Some materials like glass or clear plastic let light travel through them.* These are called **transparent**. *Other materials, like* tissue paper or thin fabric, only let *some light through* them. These are called **translucent**.

I can see clearly now

Transparent materials like glass are very useful to us in our day-to-day lives. They allow light to pass through without scattering the rays, which means we can see images through them clearly. This makes them useful for windows, lenses, or packaging when we need to see what is inside.

FACT ATTACK

See through me

Some animals have translucent body parts, making it harder for predators to catch and eat them.

Riddle me this!

We are surrounded by a transparent material all the time ... what is it?

Answer on page 28

Only outlines

Translucent material lets some light through, but it partly blocks or scatters the light rays so objects can't be seen clearly. Think of tissue paper. You can see outlines and shadows through it, but not details. Translucency often depends on how thin or thick a material is, for example paper is more translucent than card.

Reflect or absorb

Opaque materials do not let any light pass through them. They block light, either by **absorbing** or reflecting it. Shiny materials like metal foil reflect a lot of the light that hits them. Dull materials such as wood absorb the rays.

NO ENTRY

WHAT ARE SHADOWS?

WHAT ARE SHADOWS?

Shadows are made when light is blocked.

Remember how light can only travel in straight lines? When a light ray is blocked by an object, it can't bend around it, so it creates a shadow. This is a dark area the same shape as the object blocking it.

> Shadows aren't spooky unless something spooky makes them!

FACT ATTACK

Size and Shape

Shadows are always the same shape as the thing that is making them, but they aren't always the same size. Their size depends on the angle that the light is falling. This is why your shadow is short at midday when the sun is right above, but looks like it belongs to a giant at sunset, when the sun is at an angle!

Give it a go!

Create a sculpture that casts an arty shadow using random objects and bits of rubbish.

You will need:
A torch or desk lamp.
A plain wall.
A selection of objects
or bits of rubbish, e.g. toys,
bottles, etc.

What you do:
Set up your lamp so it will cast shadows on the wall. Hold the objects in front of the lamp to test out what shadows they make. Try turning and moving them around, nearer to and further from the lamp. Try to create a shadow picture on the wall by combining the shadows of your objects.

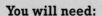

A

B

C

POP QUIZ!
Here is this boy's shadow at different times of day. One is at midday, one is in the middle of the afternoon, and one is at sunset. Which is which? **Why are they different?**
Answer on page 28.

Did you know?

Transparent objects, such as glass, let light through them so they do not have shadows.

What is reflection?

When light bounces off a surface.

When light rays hit a surface, they bounce off it and start travelling in a different direction. Some surfaces **reflect** more light than others, or reflect it in different ways. Smooth, shiny surfaces like mirrors reflect a lot of light and reflect it straight back in one direction. Uneven surfaces like crinkled foil reflect light in many directions. Even dull surfaces like wood or brick reflect some light – which is how we are able to see them.

The law of reflection

When light reflects off a flat, shiny surface like a mirror or still water, the rays bounce off at exactly the same angle as they came from. This creates clear reflected images.

Wavy wobbly

When light hits an uneven surface like crinkled foil or rippled water the rays bounce off at different angles. This creates unclear reflected images.

Reflections everywhere

We don't think of materials like
wood or fabric as being reflective, but they do
reflect some light, which is how our eyes can detect them.
Light from a source such as the sun or a lightbulb hits the
object, then some of it bounces back into our eyes,
allowing us to see the object.

Bounce Bounce Bounce

Light from the sun will
probably have bounced off lots
of different things like clouds,
buildings or furniture before it
reaches your eyes.

FACT ATTACK

Lots of fish use a mirror-effect to help
them hide from predators in open
water. Shiny silver scales reflect
their surroundings, making the fish
harder to see.

What is refraction?

When light travels through materials, it is bent.

Although light cannot change direction or go round corners by itself, light can be bent. When it moves from one transparent material to another, it changes direction slightly, or **refracts**.

POP QUIZ!

Objects seen in water often look as though they are less deep than they really are. Look at this picture. The cat sees the fish as being less deep than it really is. Why is that? Answer on page 29.

Refraction in action

One of the easiest ways to see the effect of refraction is to put something like a pencil or a straw in a glass of water, so that it is part in the water and part in the air. The object will appear bent or broken.

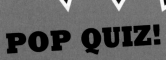

where cat sees fish

where fish really is

Slow down, speed up

Refraction occurs because even though light is super speedy, it slows down very slightly when it travels through denser materials like glass or water. It speeds up again when it passes back out into the air.

Uses of refraction

Refraction has many uses in daily life. By bending light with lenses, we can **magnify** objects, or see things much further away.

Give it a go!

See a surprising refractive effect with a glass of water. Fill up a clear glass with water. Hold the picture on this page of the girl rollerblading right behind the glass. She is facing to the left. Now slowly move the book backwards, away from the glass. She will change direction, and start skating the other way!

It's refraction action!

Colourful light

Clear, white light, like light from a torch, doesn't look colourful. But actually it is made up of all the colours of the rainbow. They are red, orange, yellow, green, pale blue, dark blue, and purple. Another name for these colours is the **visible spectrum**.

Long wave

Red light wave

Violet light wave

short wave

On a different wavelength

Remember how light travels in waves? The different colours have different wavelengths. The longest light waves that our eyes can detect are red light. Violet light has the shortest waves.

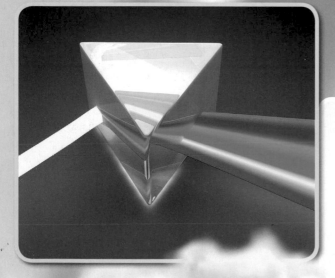

Splitting light

A beam of white light can be split into different colours by shining it through a glass **prism**. The prism refracts the different wavelengths by different amounts, splitting it into separate colours.

White light can be **filtered**, so that only some or one of the colours pass through. Use this trick to send secret messages! You will need a piece of red cellophane, a sheet of white paper, and red and blue highlighter pens.

Step 1

Draw two different pictures or write two different messages. Write or draw your real, secret message in blue. Write or draw a second, decoy message in red. Anyone who sees your letter will not know which is the real message.

Step 2

Have your friend view both messages through the red cellophane. Only the blue, secret message will be visible - the red one will have disappeared!

How it works

The red cellophane stops light of any colour except red passing through. White light (made up of all the colours) bounces off the white paper, but only the red can go through the cellophane, making the white paper look the same colour as the red writing. The blue writing reflects only blue light, which cannot pass through the filter, so it appears black.

LIGHT AND SIGHT

We use light to see.

Humans and most other animals have **evolved** eyes that use light to see the world. Some animals have very good eyesight. Others rely more on senses like smell or hearing, and so have weaker eyesight. Our eyes detect the light that bounces off objects around us. They send this information to our brains which create the pictures we see.

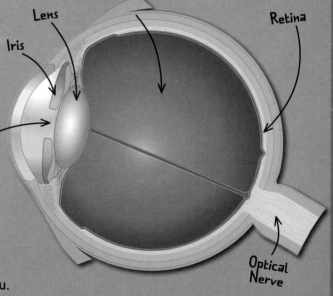

How eyes use light

Light enters your eye through the black hole called the **pupil**. It travels through a clear lens which focuses the light on an area at the back of the eye called the **retina**.

Iris

Lens

Retina

Pupil

Optical Nerve

Amazing retina

Your retina has about 130 million special cells which detect light and colour. These cells send information along a nerve to your brain, which translates the information into an image of the world around you.

Eye, Eye

Humans, like most animals have two eyes. This isn't just so we have a spare! Having two eyes means each eye has a very slightly different point of view. This helps our brain figure out how near or far an object is. This is called **depth perception**. People who are blind in one eye can sometimes struggle with tasks like driving a car or catching a ball that rely on quickly seeing distances.

Colour vision

Our eyes are very good at detecting different colours. But why do objects seem to be different colours in the first place? The reason is that when light hits an object, some of the colours in light are absorbed, and others are reflected back. We only see the reflected colours.

EYE SPY!

How many pairs of eyes can you spot?

Light and Life

Light is essential to life on earth.

Light isn't just important because we need it to see, it is essential to all living things. This is because plants need light to grow, and all other animals eat plants, or eat animals that eat plants. Without sunlight, humans wouldn't exist at all.

carbon dioxide

sunlight

water

Hungry plants

The process plants use to change energy from the sun into plant matter is called **photosynthesis**. It's basically how plants eat. They take in carbon dioxide from the air, and water from the ground. They turn these into sugar and oxygen using the energy from sunlight.

Did you know?

In Greek, photo means 'light', and synthesis means 'putting together'. So photosynthesis means 'putting things together using light'.

FACT ATTACK

Feeling green

Photosynthesis happens in a plant's leaves, which contain a special substance called 'chlorophyll'. Chlorophyll traps sunlight, and is the stuff that makes leaves green in colour. Plants try to get as much sunlight as possible, by growing big leaves, or long stems to reach towards the sun.

POP QUIZ!
This plant died after someone removed all of its leaves. **Why did it die?**

Life without sunlight

In the deepest ocean, where the ocean floor can be as much as 10 kilometres down, there is no sunlight. But amazingly, some animals still live there, feeding on stuff that drops from above - and each other! Many of the strange creatures in the deep ocean are **bioluminescent**, meaning they give off light themselves. They use their lights to attract mates, or catch prey.

Angler fish

Types of light

There are more types of light than humans can see.

The light we see with isn't the only sort of light. The bit that we can see, the visible spectrum, is just a small part of the whole **electromagnetic spectrum** of light energy. This contains **infrared** and **ultraviolet** (UV) light, which some animals can see. But it also contains **X-rays**, and radio waves.

Infrared light can be detected by special cameras, which are used for night vision.

Did you know?
Even the wavelengths of light that our eyes can't see have practical purposes.

Radio waves are used for communication and broadcasting.

Microwaves are used in microwave ovens for cooking food.

Very low frequency waves are sometimes used to contact submarines underwater.

FACT ATTACK

Super-colour

Flowers look colourful to us, but to bees they are even brighter! Bees can see UV light. UV cameras show extra patterns on some flowers' petals which act like bullseyes to guide bees to the nectar.

what we
see

bee's eye
view

Invisible numbers?

Not everyone can see all the colours in the visible spectrum. These people are called **colour blind**. Look at the two circles above. Can you read both the numbers? If not, you might be colour blind.

Visible light
is the part of the spectrum we can see. We also use it to make electricity, with solar panels.

Ultraviolet light
has a lot of uses. Blood glows under UV light, so it is used to find clues at crime scenes.

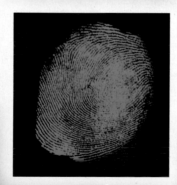

X-rays
pass through muscles and skin, but not through bone. We use them to take pictures of our bones.

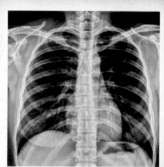

Gamma rays
are used to kill germs on medical equipment. They are very strong, and can be dangerous to our health.

25

LIGHT AND HEALTH

Light can be dangerous.

Even though we need light to stay alive, it can be dangerous to our health too. If we spend too much time in the sun, we can burn, or even develop skin cancer. The light from the sun is so powerful it can damage our eyes.

Stay safe in the sun

It's fun to play outside on a sunny day, but it's important to always wear sunscreen. That's because ultraviolet light from the sun can cause our skin to burn. Without protection, our skin can turn red and sore, then blister and peel off - yuck!

POP QUIZ!

Which of these things should you do to stay safe in the sunshine?

2 **wear sunglasses**

3 **eat fruit**

6 **do exercise**

4 **drink water**

5 **wear a hat**

1 **wear sunscreen**

See the power of the sun by making sun prints! You will need a sheet of dark-coloured construction paper (also called 'sugar paper', blue or black works best), some masking tape, some card (such as an old cereal packet), a sunny window and a pair of scissors.

Step 1

Cut shapes out of your card and stick them onto the sheet of construction paper using little loops of masking tape. These card shapes will temporarily block the sun from hitting the construction paper, but will be removed afterwards.

Step 2

Once you have created a design you are happy with, tape the sheet up in a sunny window. Leave the paper up for a couple of days (how long the process takes will depend on how much sun you get).

Step 3

After a couple of days of strong sunshine, take the sheet down, and remove the card shapes. The sun should have **bleached** the space around the card, creating a sun-printed design.

And the answer is ...

Page 5

Pop quiz: sound waves are not a type of light.

Page 6

Find the light: there are 6 light sources. The street lamp, firefly, the television, the lamp, the phone screen, and the candle. The moon and the candle reflection are NOT light sources.

Page 11

Riddle me this: the transparent material that surrounds us is the air!

Page 13

Pop quiz: A is at sunset, B is the middle of the afternoon, and C is midday. The midday shadow is the shortest because the sun is directly above, and the sunset shadow is the longest because the sun is shining from the side.

Page 16

Pop quiz: the fish looks less deep than it really is because the light rays bend as they pass from the water to the air. The cat's eyes follow the rays as though they are travelling in a straight line, making it look as through the fish is nearer the surface.

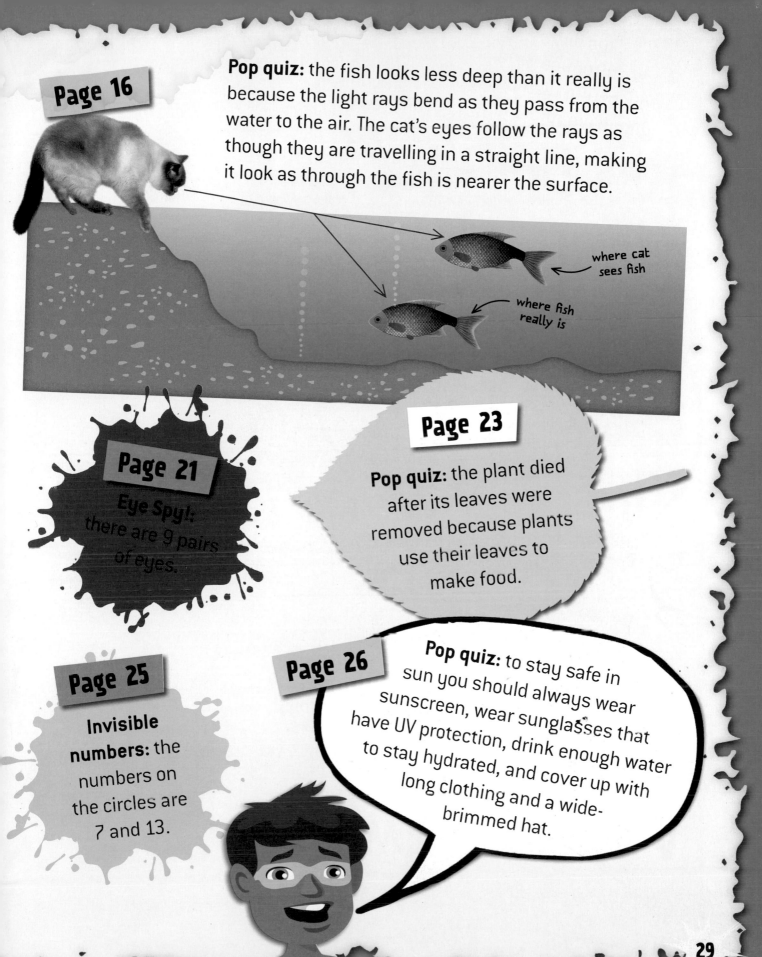

where cat sees fish

where fish really is

Page 21

Eye Spy!: there are 9 pairs of eyes.

Page 23

Pop quiz: the plant died after its leaves were removed because plants use their leaves to make food.

Page 25

Invisible numbers: the numbers on the circles are 7 and 13.

Page 26

Pop quiz: to stay safe in sun you should always wear sunscreen, wear sunglasses that have UV protection, drink enough water to stay hydrated, and cover up with long clothing and a wide-brimmed hat.

Glossary

Absorb (light) To take in light energy, rather than bouncing it back or letting it pass through

Bioluminescence A type of light given off by living things

Bleached Made paler in colour

Colour blind When a person's eyes can't detect all the colours in the rainbow

Depth perception The ability that humans and some other animals have to see in 3D

Electromagnetic radiation A scientific term for light

Electromagnetic spectrum The full range of wavelengths of light, including types of light that humans can't see

Evolve Develop over millions of years

Filter To let some wavelengths of light through, but block others

Gamma rays The type of light with the shortest wavelength

Infrared light A type of light with longer wavelengths than visible light

Magnify Make something look bigger

Microwave A type of light used by microwave ovens to cook food

Opaque A word to describe material that does not let any light through

Photon A tiny bit of light energy

Photosynthesis The process plants use to make light energy into food

Prism A pyramid or wedge-shaped piece of glass or plastic that can be used to split light into separate colours

Pupil The little black hole in the middle of the eye that lets light through

Reflect Bouncing light off a surface

Refract Bend light by passing it through one material into to another

Retina The light-detecting area at the back of the eye

Transparent A word to describe material that lets all light through

Translucent A word to describe material that lets some light through

Ultraviolet light A type of light with a shorter wavelength than visible light

Visible spectrum The part of the electromagnetic spectrum that our eyes can naturally see

X-ray A type of light with a shorter wavelength than visible light

Further reading

Disgusting and Dreadful Science:
Glaring Light and Other Eye-Burning Rays
Anna Claybourne (Franklin Watts, 2013

Science Secrets: Secrets of Light
Anna Claybourne (Franklin Watts, 2014)

How Does Science Work: Light
Carol Ballard (Wayland, 2014)

Mind Webs: Light and Sound
Anna Claybourne (Wayland, 2014)

Moving Up With Science: Light
Peter Riley (Watts, 2015)

Websites

www.explainthatstuff.com/light.html
A simple explanation of what light is, where it comes from, and how it behaves in our world.

www.bbc.co.uk/bitesize/ks2/science/physical_processes/light/read/1/
Read about light and try a quiz to test your knowledge

www.sciencekids.co.nz/light.html
A site with games, videos, and facts all about light.

www.exploratorium.edu/snacks/collection/color
Lots of projects and activities exploring light and colour.

Index